tierney gearon

alphabet book

a

airplane adventure

b

bear boy

c

clown car

d

doubtful dangers

e

eagle eye

f

forgetful fishing

g

grumpy girls

h

hollow house

i
instant incognito

j

jumping joy

k

kissing kids

long leg lollipops

mister mustache

n

naughty nurse

o

obviously old

p

private princess

q

quiet quiver

r

rat reading

s

sunbeam stones

t

tree twins

u

ultimate uniform

V

vacuum vacation

W

wonder wig

X

xmas xing

y

yelling yellow

z

zany zeal

Tierney Gearon - Alphabet Book

This book is a friend and family collaboration all
of the images were taken from July 2010 - July 2013.

Thanks Alexander, Bailey, Charlotte, Christie, Fiona, Grace, Izzy,
Joe, Levi, Lindy, Lucas, Mia, Sky, Sonny, Violet, & Walker.

© Damiani 2013
© Photographs, Tierney Gearon

Photography - Tierney Gearon
Design - Richard Harrington
Image Production - Allan Finamore, Epilogue inc

DAMIANI

Damiani
via Zanardi, 376
40131 Bologna, Italy
t. +39 051 63 56 811
f. +39 051 63 47 188
info@damianieditore.com
www.damianieditore.com

Printed in July 2013 by Grafiche Damiani, Bologna, Italy.

ISBN 978-88-6208-320-1